IMAGES
of America

JACKSON'S
NORTH STATE STREET

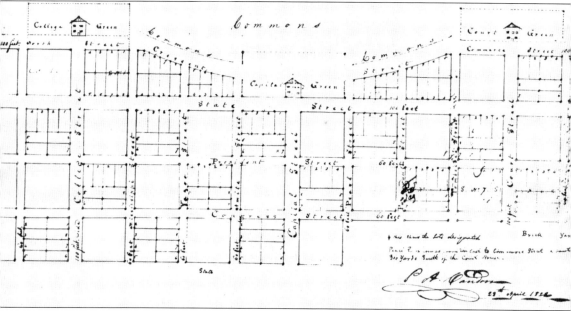

This map shows the original layout of Jackson as platted in 1820–1821 by commissioner Peter Van Dorn, based on a suggestion made by Pres. Thomas Jefferson as a way to expand New Orleans. His suggestion was to use a chessboard as the basis for a city, with the black squares being developed and the white squares remaining as undeveloped wilderness or landscaped as parks or groves. Also visible on this map are the names of the first streets in Jackson. The broadest streets running east to west are, from north to south, College Street, Capitol Street, and Court Street. All three of these were to terminate at their eastern end at a college or school, the capitol building, and a courthouse. The other east-to-west streets were named after the rivers that ran through the state of Mississippi, namely, from north to south, Mississippi, Yazoo, Amite, Pearl, Pascagoula, and Tombigbee Streets. The north-to-south streets are Congress, President, and State Streets. (Mississippi Department of Archives and History.)

ON THE COVER: State Street has long been the main parade route through downtown Jackson. This photograph, taken on December 9, 1948, shows the Christmas parade as it winds past the 100 block of North State Street. (LeFleur's Bluff Heritage Foundation.)

IMAGES
of America

JACKSON'S
NORTH STATE STREET

Todd Sanders

ARCADIA
PUBLISHING

Copyright © 2009 by Todd Sanders
ISBN 978-0-7385-6802-7

Published by Arcadia Publishing
Charleston SC, Chicago IL, Portsmouth NH, San Francisco CA

Printed in the United States of America

Library of Congress Control Number: 2008938934

For all general information contact Arcadia Publishing at:
Telephone 843-853-2070
Fax 843-853-0044
E-mail sales@arcadiapublishing.com
For customer service and orders:
Toll-Free 1-888-313-2665

Visit us on the Internet at www.arcadiapublishing.com

To Nanci, my wife and best friend.

CONTENTS

ACKNOWLEDGMENTS

This project could not have been possible without the support and encouragement of my wife, Nanci, and my three wonderful children, Tice, Becca Jane, and Rachel Claire. I would also like to thank my parents, Joe and Diana Sanders, and my mother-in-law, Janet Johnson, for their help.

In addition, I would like to thank Richard Cawthon, former chief architectural historian with the historic preservation division of the Mississippi Department of Archives and History, for his friendship and guidance. Many of the discussions we have had over the years on the architectural history of Jackson have found their way into this book. I would also like to thank Jennifer Baughn, current chief architectural historian with the historic preservation division of the Mississippi Department of Archives and History, for her support of this project. I also appreciate the help of the staff in the archives division of the Mississippi Department of Archives and History. Elaine Owens, Ann Webster, Clinton Bagley, Preston Everette, Grady Howell, Joyce Dixon, and Nancy Bounds all provided much appreciated support, encouragement, and ideas. Unless otherwise noted, courtesies to the Mississippi Department of Archives and History are listed as MDAH.

I want to thank Helen Rotwein for allowing me to use so many wonderful images from the collection of LeFleur's Bluff Heritage Foundation. Unless otherwise noted, courtesies to LeFleur's Bluff Heritage Foundation are listed as LBHF. Thanks also go to Mattie Sink, manuscripts coordinator at Mississippi State University. Mrs. Dean Alexander, Mrs. Robert B. (Susan) Mims, and Mrs. Samuel Fletcher King all receive special thanks for the use of historic photographs of their family homes. Thanks also go to Edward L. Blake and the Mississippi Farm Bureau. I also want to thank the faculty and staff of St. Andrew's Episcopal School as well as the entire congregation of St. Andrew's for their assistance. I also want to give a special word of thanks to Mary Carol Miller, who, in addition to sharing with me her research on North State Street, gave me many words of support and encouragement. To her also goes a huge thank-you for reading my first draft.

Finally, I would like to thank my editor at Arcadia Publishing, Katie Stephens, for her patience, guidance, and support.

INTRODUCTION

Almost from the beginning, Jackson's North State Street has been the location of some of the community's premier residences. Starting in the block or so north of the c. 1840 State Capitol Building, now known as the Old Capitol Museum, North State Street was lined by stately homes of many different styles and periods, from rather simple antebellum cottages to grand Greek Revival, elaborate Queen Anne, romantic Colonial Revival, and stately Classical Revival mansions.

For generations, North State Street was home to many civic, business, and cultural leaders. State legislators, U.S. senators, prominent clergymen, bankers, lawyers, and businessmen all made their homes here, each putting on display the tangible evidence of their success in life for the benefit of the public as they walked by, rode the streetcar, or paraded in their horse-drawn carriages and later in their automobiles. Indeed, many citizens made a Sunday outing of walking up and down the street, enjoying the beauty of the architecture of the town.

Sharing this grand promenade with these fine homes were many imposing institutional complexes. In addition to the c. 1840 state capitol, which anchors the southern end of North State Street, the State of Mississippi constructed, or in some cases acquired and repurposed, complexes of buildings in an attempt to meet the special needs of some of its citizens. Among these were institutions for the blind, deaf, and dumb, and the insane, as well as the indigent. Also the Mississippi Baptist Convention took over and expanded a small hospital into a major medical center complex. Churches, a public school, and eventually the city library joined the parade.

Sadly, this beautiful street fell prey, as so many have, to the mundane needs of commerce, and many of these stately homes, erected by their proud owners who no doubt intended for them to serve as a center for gracious living for generations, were demolished. Apartment buildings, ever-expanding hospitals, office blocks, retail establishments, parking lots, government buildings, and church complexes went up in their place. In fact, the highest concentration of surviving 19th-century houses on North State Street, just four in number, are found three blocks north of the Old Capitol. Included in this grouping, which is listed as a National Register of Historic Places district, are two of Jackson's half a dozen or so surviving antebellum houses, an elegant Queen Anne mansion, and a grand double-galleried Classical Revival house. Unfortunately, this picturesque reminder of what State Street had been has now been surrounded by parking lots and auxiliary buildings for a local church.

This book will discuss the fate of many of these lovely homes. Included will be images from the Works Progress Administration (WPA) taken during the Great Depression of the 1930s, when the streets character first began to change. Contrasted with this will be postcard views from the late 19th and early 20th centuries that show the street in all its glory. Many images in the book were taken by the City of Jackson itself as it worked to improve the transportation needs of the physical street and inadvertently captured wonderful images of several of the houses, buildings, and citizens who made up the life of the street. There are also photographs taken by state and local preservationists in early attempts to chronicle this grand street as it disappeared around them. Perhaps the most captivating images are family snapshots taken in celebration of some now unknown event or to document an unexpected March snowstorm.

In short, this book will be a fond remembrance for longtime Jacksonians of the true beauty of a now largely lost part of their city, as well as a call to arms to preservationists to never take anything, no matter how permanent and settled it may seem, for granted. It can all be lost seemingly overnight.

One

THE EARLY YEARS

The very first capital of the young state of Mississippi, which entered the union as the 20th state on December 10, 1817, was located in Natchez. After moving the capital from Natchez back to the territorial capital of Washington, then back to Natchez and eventually to Columbia for a year, the state government, in 1821, commissioned three men—Thomas Hinds, William Lattimore, and Peter Van Dorn—to locate a site near the geographical center of the state for a new capital city. This idea, grounded in the concept of Jeffersonian democracy, followed a pattern established by many older East Coast states to remove the seat of government away from the corrupt influence of wealthy planters and merchants.

The Treaty of Doak's Stand, signed in 1820 between the U.S. government and the Choctaw Indians, resulted in the cession of 5.5 million acres of land. The commissioners decided on a location, within the cession, known as LeFleur's Bluff. This site was a former ferry crossing on the Pearl River, 20 feet above the floodplain with an abundant supply of timber and water. Although this location was outside the 35-mile radius from the actual center of the state, the government did accept the site and named it in honor of the hero of the Battle of New Orleans, Maj. Gen. Andrew Jackson.

The town was not an immediate success. Jackson was, as many people apparently believed, located near the state's geographical center so that it could be equally inconvenient for everybody. Other than those who absolutely had to be there, few people moved to Jackson in its first decade. Consequently, it remained a small settlement. In fact, it almost ceased to exist entirely and probably would have had not the Constitutional Convention of 1832 mandated that the legislature meet in Jackson through 1850. With its existence guaranteed for at least 18 more years, the state began to invest in the construction of permanent buildings to house the government, most notably the state capitol, located on Capitol Green where Capitol Street intersects State Street.

Facing down Capitol Street from its intersection with State Street, the *c.* 1840 Old Capitol is Jackson's most historic structure. This Greek Revival building was designed by English émigré architect William Nichols. As was typical for Greek Revival structures, this brick building was originally covered in stucco that was then scored, or the surface cut with fake masonry joints, in imitation of stone. This stucco treatment was only applied to the facade, or western elevation, and the northern and southern ends. The rear elevation, which faced onto the Pearl River swamp, was never covered with stucco but remained bare brick. The arches were added in a major building rehabilitation in 1870–1871. Also visible in this early photograph is the *c.* 1846 wrought-iron and limestone fence that stretched across the front of the building from Amite Street to Pearl Street. (MDAH.)

This view, taken from the roof of the Old Capitol and looking west, is part of the well-known panoramic photograph of downtown Jackson made by E. Von Seutter in 1869. Visible in the right foreground is the low pitched, hipped roof of the building known for many years as Spengler's Corner. This building was constructed around 1840 on the northeastern corner of State and Capitol Streets. Originally a one-story brick commercial building, Spengler's Corner was enlarged sometime before the Civil War to a full two stories in height. This structure, Jackson's oldest extant commercial building, has served many uses over the years, including saloon, hotel, drugstore, and offices. From this view, one can see how small and rural a community Jackson was after almost half a century of existence. This rural character would continue to define Jackson for many more years. (MDAH.)

The five-story brick Bowman House, constructed around 1857 at the northwest corner of State and Amite Streets, was described as the largest and most commodious hotel in the state and contained between 85 and 100 rooms, with accommodations for 300 people, including servants. The occasion for the May 1, 1860, photograph was the volunteer fire company celebration. The large group in the center of the photograph is all members of the fire company. They are gathered in front of the volunteer Jackson Fire Company building, the two-story brick structure visible at right. Volunteer fire companies provided fire protection for Jackson prior to the establishment of the City Fire Department in 1904. Visible behind the group is a wooden stile, or steps, allowing access over the wooden picket fence that enclosed the grounds of the Capitol Green on the northern and southern ends. (MDAH.)

The Bowman House burned on June 9, 1863. The hotel was never rebuilt, and the ruins stood until 1874. Visible in the background (at right) is the northern end of the Old Capitol. On the corner of State and Amite Streets can be clearly seen the white painted picket fence along the Amite Street side and the wrought-iron fence along State Street. Also visible, just to the left of the ruins, is the roof of the firehouse. The photograph below, part of the Von Seutter panorama of 1869, shows the ruins from the roof of the Old Capitol. Also visible in this photograph is North State Street as it runs off to the north, showing again that Jackson was a rural community at the time. (Both MDAH.)

Farewell View of the Old Presbyterian Church.
JACKSON, MISS.
TAKEN ON MONDAY AFTERNOON, JULY 20, 1891.

The photograph above, another view from the 1869 Von Seutter panorama, shows the steeple, roof, and pediment of the First Presbyterian Church. This building, constructed around 1846 on the northwest corner of State and Yazoo Streets, was one of the first substantial edifices erected in the young town for the use of a religious group. The design of the elegant brick Greek Revival building has been attributed to William Nichols, the architect of the Old Capitol. The photograph at left, taken on July 20, 1891, as a farewell to the nearly 50-year-old building, clearly shows the elegant treatment of the facade. Shortly after this photograph was made, the building was demolished and replaced by a larger Gothic Revival structure that occupied this site for 60 more years, giving the Presbyterians a presence on this corner for over 100 years. (Both MDAH.)

The Old Robinson House, formerly located at 326 North State Street, was constructed around 1850. As was often the case with the first houses constructed along North State Street, this house and accompanying grounds and outbuildings occupied virtually the entire block. Like so many houses of the antebellum period, the house appears to have originally consisted of a center hall with two rooms on each side. The trim surrounding the door and windows on the front porch is in one of the popular variations of the familiar Greek Revival style popular in antebellum Mississippi. The house was enlarged and remodeled many times over the years as needs dictated and fortunes allowed. The purchase and installation of the decorative ironwork on the house was documented in a September 2, 1945, article from the Jackson *Clarion Ledger* about the house's impending demolition. According to this article, the owner purchased and installed the ironwork in 1876. This grand residence stood where the Welty Library parking lot is now. (MDAH.)

The Hilzheim-Ledbetter House, formerly located at 426 North State Street, was constructed around 1850. This grand brick Greek Revival house was one of the largest houses built in antebellum Jackson. Not surprisingly, William Nichols has been mentioned as the possible architect for this house. Certainly the impressive Ionic columns of the full-width colonnade are reminiscent of Nichols's designs for the Old Capitol and the Lyceum at the University of Mississippi. Furthermore, the design of the balcony railing above the front door is very similar in design to the balcony railing at the Governor's Mansion, which was designed by Nichols and completed in 1842. It certainly stands to reason that Nichols, one of the most prominent architects in the state and probably the only such professional in Jackson at the time, would have been involved in the design and construction of one of the city's grandest residences. (MDAH.)

The Clifton-Burwell House, located at 500 North State Street, is one of the approximately half dozen antebellum houses extant in the city of Jackson. The property on which the house stands was purchased by one of Jackson's early citizens, William Morris, in August 1848 for $400. Since the same property was sold by his estate in February 1851 for $2,300, a construction date of 1849–1850 can be safely given. Also, given this date, this house may be the oldest extant private residence in the city. This house is a good example of the typical center hall, double pile plan so popular throughout antebellum Mississippi. In fact, except for the upper half story, the original section of the Old Robinson House, which stood at 326 North State Street, was probably quite similar to this structure. The current Colonial Revival porch columns, balustrade, and dormer windows were added in an early-20th-century remodeling. (MDAH.)

The Virden-Patton House, located at 512 North State Street, is another of the approximately half dozen antebellum houses extant in Jackson. According to *Jackson Landmarks*, compiled and published by the Jackson Junior League in 1982, the Virden-Patton House was constructed around 1850, approximately the same date as the Clifton-Burwell House next door, for James Wilson. Wilson was a painter who had the contract to paint both the Governor's Mansion and city hall. Wilson, however, never lived in the house, and it was sold instead to Alexander Virden, a prominent local merchant. The Virden-Patton House has retained more of its original design than the Clifton-Burwell House. The Virden-Patton House, a brick, story-and-a-half, Greek Revival galleried cottage, still has its original square columns. Square columns, like those used here, were common on antebellum Mississippi houses not just on smaller cottages, but also on many larger residences as well. (MDAH.)

The Nugent-Shands House was formerly located at 607 North State Street. Although apparently built around 1840, this house was heavily remodeled in the Classical Revival style in the late 19th or early 20th century. According to a newspaper article written by Anabel Power and published in the *Jackson Daily News* on June 2, 1946, this brick and stone house originally had square columns, which were replaced with the elegant, round, fluted, Corinthian ones seen in the photograph. In 1916, a fire damaged the top of the house, but the solid brick walls were not seriously damaged. It seems likely, given the appearance of the house in the photograph and the record of the 1916 fire, that the exterior of the house was extensively redesigned after the fire. Possibly this redesign was influenced by the new state capitol, a grand Beaux-Arts structure completed in 1903 and visible from the Nugent-Shands House. (MDAH.)

Formerly located at 653 North State Street, the *c.* 1855 E. L. Herring House is a good example of the vernacular Greek Revival cottages common in antebellum Jackson. The round columns on the front porch are later replacements. The original square, paneled columns resembled the pilasters, which are still visible where the porch roof meets the wall of the house. (MDAH.)

The Yerger Mansion, a substantial 15-room house with grounds occupying most of the 700 block of North State Street, was erected around 1850. The original Greek Revival mansion is visible between the trees. The estate was acquired for the Deaf and Dumb Institute in 1872 and was subsequently enlarged and remodeled. The complex burned in 1902, and a new school was built elsewhere. (MDAH.)

E. von Seutter, in addition to being Jackson's most memorable 19th-century photographer, was also a resident of North State Street. His home, pictured here, was known as Ivy Cottage, presumably in homage to the elegant and elaborate gardens surrounding it. The distinguished-looking gentleman in the photograph is believed to be E. von Seutter. (MDAH.)

Another example of an earlier house with later architectural embellishments is the Kirkpatrick House. This elegant cottage, originally a simple *c.* 1850 Greek Revival cottage, was dressed up with fanciful jigsaw work spanning the area between the tops of the square-paneled columns and the soffit and a substantial early-20th-century Colonial Revival balustrade. This house stood at 935 North State Street. (MDAH.)

Formerly located at 952 North State Street, the Fearn-Anderson House was among the largest and grandest of the antebellum Greek Revival residences lining this street. Architecturally, this house employs a typical Mississippi Greek Revival treatment in the use of two-story square columns in its portico, reflecting the more traditional vernacular approach to the style. While William Nichols, a British-trained architect, was the probable designer of the Hilzheim House, which stood in the 400 block of North State Street, the Fearn-Anderson House was probably designed and built by its owner with the assistance of a local master builder. Perhaps this is somehow appropriate given the fact that this house was constructed just south of what is today known as Fortification Street and in the 1850s was the outskirts of town, if not in the country outright, while the Hilzheim House was built much closer to the center of town. (MDAH.)

Constructed around 1870 in a transitional Greek Revival/Italianate style, this cottage was known as the Eckles House. In 1910, the forerunner of Jackson's Baptist Hospital was opened in this house. In 1913, it was moved a short distance to the east from its original location at 1120 North State Street to make room for the construction of a new, much larger hospital facility. (MDAH.)

This Greco Italianate cottage appears to be the house known as Elsinore, which, according to *Jackson Landmarks*, was where the Millsaps College library now stands. Built around 1850, and rebuilt after an 1860s fire, this part of the house sat atop a brick-raised basement. In the 1920s, the frame upper story (seen here) was moved farther north on campus, and the lower brick portion was demolished. (MDAH.)

The Mississippi Lunatic Asylum was originally located where the sprawling campus of the University Medical Center is today. According to *The Story of Jackson*, the state legislature in March 1848 decreed that a lunatic asylum was to be established near or in the city of Jackson. The original site, a lot containing 5 acres near downtown, was determined to be too small, so this site containing 140 acres and located approximately 2 miles north of Jackson was acquired. Construction began in late 1848. The asylum was completed and opened for patients in January 1855. For its time, the asylum was a modern structure employing gas lighting and steam heat. (MDAH.)

Two

THE GOLDEN AGE

Despite the fact that Jackson was not totally reduced to ashes by the conquering Union army, the small city did suffer setbacks, as did most of the South. Most of the damage inflicted on the community occurred in the southern and western parts of town nearer the railroad. One major loss to North State Street during the war was the burning of the Bowman Hotel in 1863. As with most burning of buildings during the war, Southerners like to blame the invading Yankees. However, in this case, it is not known for certain how the fire started. At any rate, the ruins remained on the corner of North State and Amite Streets for many years after the war to serve as a constant reminder of the recent hostilities.

Despite the economic and physical damage, recovery began rather quickly. In 1871, Jackson saw the construction of its first street railway or trolley system. This trolley, originally consisting of cars pulled by mules, ran down Capitol Street from the Capitol Building to the depot on the western end of downtown. The railway soon extended up North State Street to Fortification Street. The name of this street served as another constant reminder of the late unpleasantness since this street was the general location of the Confederate fortifications that guarded the city during the war and was effectively the edge of town.

The trolley system allowed for the construction of houses farther away from the central part of the city, and soon many of Jackson's business leaders built fine homes farther up North State Street. The period after the close of Reconstruction through World War I saw the construction of the largest and grandest homes ever to grace the street. In 1903, the new capitol was constructed in what is often called the Beaux-Arts style, a highly sophisticated, classical architecture. This influential building no doubt inspired many residents to build their new homes in a grand classical style.

This c. 1920 image of the Old Capitol shows the building after it had been converted into a state office building. After the state government moved into the elegant new capitol in 1903, the old building was allowed to sit and deteriorate for more than a decade as debate went on as to what to do with it. The building did see minimal use during this period as part of the state fairgrounds, which are just down the bluff behind the building. Finally, about 1916, the decision was made to renovate the 76-year-old structure into a state office building. The handsome wrought-iron and stone fence had been removed at some point prior to the beginning of the renovation. The circular window in the center of the pediment apparently replaced a rusted clock face. The clock is believed to have been installed in the late 1840s. (MDAH.)

This view of the southern end of the Old Capitol shows the damage inflicted to the building by a hurricane in September 1909. According to an article in the *Washington Post* dated September 21, 1909, a large portion of the roof was ripped off of the building and carried many yards away. In addition to this, many windows were broken, including those in the cupola. (MDAH.)

This view of the northern end of the Old Capitol shows the damage inflicted to the cupola by the hurricane. Also shown in this photograph are the ticket booths, which provided access to the state fairgrounds. Thus the Old Capitol, once the largest and grandest building in the state, was reduced to an exhibit building for the state fair. (MDAH.)

The loss of large parts of its roof and many windows exposed the interior of the neglected old building to the weather. To add insult to injury, no repairs were made for seven years. This exacerbated the damage the building had already suffered from years of deferred maintenance and faulty foundations. These c. 1915 photographs show the deplorable condition of the interior. The Senate Chamber, seen here, still has the noble air given it by architect William Nichols many years before despite the decay. The holes in the columns had once accommodated gas sconces. The large doors seen in the photograph above had glass panes in the upper half to allow light into the inner corridors and permitted the public to see into the chamber. (Both MDAH.)

This photograph of the original dome of the Senate Chamber shows not only the damage to the plasterwork, but also an early lighting device. The fixture in the center of the ceiling was a gas light reflector. This device, added in the renovations of 1871, reflected, magnified, and focused the light generated by the gasolier that hung below it. (MDAH.)

The House Chamber, seen below in a photograph taken shortly after the government moved out in 1903, is in much better condition than it would be a decade later. Clearly visible are the gasoliers that lit the room and the stoves that heated it. The gas lighting system, first installed in the building in the late 1850s, was expanded and improved in 1871. (MDAH.)

The Confederate Monument, the largest confederate monument in the state, is located in Confederate Park, the southern end of Capitol Green. The monument was dedicated on June 3, 1891, Jefferson Davis's birthday. Originally a large statue of Jefferson Davis was included as part of the monument. The statue was removed and placed in the Old Capitol in 1922 to protect it from vandalism. (MDAH.)

This late-19th-century photograph provides a unique view of Spengler's Corner looking northeast from Capitol Street to State Street. Spengler's Corner, constructed around 1840 and enlarged with a second floor about 1850, is shown here with the elaborate cast-iron awning added to the building around 1880. The gentleman in the buggy was apparently the sheriff of Hinds County. (MDAH.)

Taken from the balcony of the Old Capitol in 1923, this photograph shows the c. 1880 cast-iron awning on Spengler's Corner as well as the wooden second-floor balcony added a few years later. The intersection of State and Capitol Streets is probably the most photographed intersection in Jackson. Consequently, the changes to Spengler's Corner over the years have been well documented. (LBHF.)

This photograph of Spengler's Corner, also from the early 1920s, shows more clearly the second-floor balcony that ran along the entire State Street facade of the building. At this time, based on the painted sign on the first-floor wall, the structure housed a drugstore. The dark lines across the photograph are cracks in the original glass negative. (LBHF.)

As mentioned earlier, the intersection of State and Capitol Streets is probably the most photographed intersection in Jackson. This photograph was made after 1935, the year the streetcar system was replaced by city buses and the tracks removed. Spengler's Corner has lost its late-19th-century balconies. Visible again are its original six-over-six, double-hung windows on the second floor. Hemphill's Drugs is the tenant. (LBHF.)

While State Street was primarily a residential street until the mid-20th century, the first block has always been a predominantly commercial block. This 1920s photograph shows the buildings in the center of this block in use as the Tucker Printing Company. (MDAH.)

The roof of the Old Capitol has provided a much sought after vantage point for photographers for many years. This photograph, taken from the same perspective as that of E. Von Seutter approximately 60 years before, shows a greatly changed Jackson. The dome of the 1903 capitol is visible in the distance. (MDAH.)

Taken in July 1932, this photograph shows the intersection of Amite and North State Streets. The building on the far right is the Standard Oil Company building standing where the Bowman House stood from 1857 to 1863. Note that the Old Capitol Green is completely without fencing of any kind, giving the area an open, urban park-like setting. (LBHF.)

As the automobile rose to prominence, the need for service stations grew. In 1932, three of the four corners at the intersection of Amite and North State Streets were occupied by service stations. The one above is almost like a commercial building sitting right on the sidewalk. Customers would drive their automobiles off the street and into the building for service. The service station in the photograph below is a more typical service station set back from the sidewalk with a freestanding canopy. Both of these service stations, gone today, were built about 1930. A third service station was located across the street from the Texaco station as part of the Standard Oil Building, shown in a photograph on page 86. (Both LBHF.)

Immediately north of the Texaco station, and formerly located on the northwest corner of Amite and North State Streets, the residential area of North State Street began. From this point north to Fortification Street, North State Street was a predominantly residential street. These two houses, today the site of a parking lot, were constructed in the late 19th and early 20th centuries. The two-story house on the right with the two-story porch is the Henry Bailey House, built in 1894. The two-story house to its left with the one-story porch was constructed around 1910. (Both LBHF.)

The Daniel Wilkinson House, which stood at 204 North State Street, the northeast corner of North State and Amite Streets, was constructed in 1904. Located on the site occupied by the Bowman House from 1857 to 1863, the Wilkinson House was easily one of the most distinctive houses ever constructed in Jackson. The architect for the house was apparently Theodore C. Link, the architect for the new state capitol. The Renaissance Revival–style mansion was architecturally distinguished by a three-story tower with its top floor open to the air. Unfortunately, the house did not remain on this site for long. The property was sold in the early 1920s to Standard Oil. By 1927, its local headquarters, which included a service station on the State Street elevation, stood on this site. The house, however, was donated to the city and was subsequently moved down the hill to the fairgrounds, where it served as the Women's Pavilion for a number of years. (MDAH.)

Dedicated on May 14, 1893, this structure served as the second home of the First Presbyterian Church in Jackson. This building, which was located at 301 North State Street, the northwest corner of Yazoo and North State Streets, stood where the former Jackson Municipal Library stands today. This church was constructed on the site of the *c.* 1846 Greek Revival–style building apparently designed by William Nichols. The first church on this site was demolished in 1891 when construction began on this handsome Gothic Revival edifice. According to Richard J. Cawthon, from the text of a proposed book, "Lost Churches of Mississippi" (not yet published), the architect for the new church was Reuben Harrison Hunt of Chattanooga, Tennessee, a regionally prominent architect who designed numerous churches, schools, and governmental buildings throughout the South from the 1880s through the 1920s. The Hunt-designed building served the needs of the congregation for another 60 years. (MDAH.)

As seen in this photograph of the intersection of North State and Yazoo Streets taken on April 24, 1930, the character of North State Street quickly changed from the more business orientation at the intersection of Amite and North State Streets just one block south to a quiet residential feel. This is the view looking east from the First Presbyterian Church. Notice the streetcar tracks. (LBHF.)

Another street scene shows some interesting pedestrian activity. Apparently this photograph shows a group of students from Millsaps College commenting on the suffrage movement. Notice the streetcar tracks going down the center of the street and the smaller street trees, including the ones behind our demonstrators, with the protective cribbing around them. No doubt many such activities took place over the years. (Mrs. Dean Morris Alexander.)

These photographs, taken from the intersection of North State and College Streets looking southeast, show the *c.* 1850 Hilzheim-Ledbetter House and the *c.* 1890 Hooker House. Very little is known about the Hooker House despite the fact that it was home to Col. Charles E. Hooker, a distinguished Confederate veteran who later became a Congressman. The Hilzheim House was victim to an unsympathetic conversion into apartments in the 1920s, when the impressive Ionic columns were removed and the entrance was relocated to the northern elevation. Some time later, a commercial building was erected to the west of the house occupying the original front lawn. Both houses were demolished for commercial purposes. Today the site is occupied by one of the many buildings of Jackson's First Baptist Church. (Above, MDAH; below, Mrs. Dean Morris Alexander.)

The Joseph Henry Morris House, 505 North State Street, was constructed around 1893. According to the National Register nomination for this property, the residence was designed by an unknown New York architect and was one of the first Classical Revival houses built in Jackson. This house is a particularly elegant example of the style, with its two-tiered gallery of modified Ionic columns that wraps around the facade and southern elevation. The above photograph, dated around 1900, shows the elaborate balustrade that originally crowned the low pitched, hipped roof. The remarkable entrance and surround contain elaborate leaded-glass windows. Projecting out from the second-floor gallery above the entrance is a small balconet supported by radiating console brackets with a pendant. (Above, Mrs. Dean Morris Alexander; left, MDAH.)

The interior of the Morris House is as elaborate and intricately finished as the facade. The photograph above shows the elegant stair hall separated from the front hall by an elegant arched screen of scroll and spindled millwork. The parlor, seen below, is an elegant room, its architecture ably matched by its elegant family furnishings, many of them Morris family heirlooms. The Morris family, one of Jackson's oldest families, first arrived in Jackson in 1837 when the family patriarch, William Powell Morris, moved here from Clinton. The current Morris home was constructed directly in front of the family's first Greek Revival residence. Morris is credited with opening the first bank in the city. His son, Joseph Henry Morris, in addition to many other business and real estate ventures, opened the first ice plant in the state in 1880. (Both MDAH.)

The Sims-Alexander House, located at 513 North State Street, was, according to the National Register of Historic Places, constructed around 1905. This imposing house is designed in what is often referred to as the Queen Anne Free Classic style. This style combines classically inspired details, seen here in the Ionic collonettes of the porches, with the irregularity of form and shape most commonly associated with the Queen Anne style, such as the steep roof, projecting gable, and round corner tower. The photograph below of the main stair shows the elegantly finished interior. Dr. Walter Scott Sims, the builder of the house, a Mississippi native, was the state's first eye, ear, nose, and throat specialist. He was also instrumental in establishing the Mississippi Blind Institute and was one of its superintendents. (Both MDAH.)

This house was constructed around 1900 by Z. D. Davis. Later generations knew it as Mrs. Lynn Carroll's house. This grand Classical Revival residence, formerly located at 529 North State Street, was distinguished by a prominent Corinthian order colonnade, which expanded into a circular pavilion at the northern end. This photograph was taken after a March 1940 snowstorm. (MDAH.)

Formerly located at 618 North State Street, this c. 1880 Italianate house was for many years the McWillie Home. An article from the April 29, 1954, *Jackson Daily News*, in describing the purchase of this property by Mrs. A. W. Horrell for her photography studio, stated, "It is another indication of the extension of the downtown retail business area . . . on State Street." (LBHF.)

The Millsaps-Buie House, located at 628 North State Street, was completed around 1888 for Maj. Reuben Webster Millsaps. This photograph, taken after a snowstorm, shows the house as it was originally constructed. The Millsaps-Buie House was designed in the most popular mode of the day, the Queen Anne style. This house is distinguished by the hallmarks of that style, which include steep roofs with varied roof lines, attached towers, turned and jig-sawn wooden decorative elements such as posts, brackets, and balustrades, decorative wooden shingles, paneled brick work in the chimneys, and stained glass. Another feature used on the Millsaps-Buie House but not always found on other Mississippi houses built in the Queen Anne style is the contrasting paint scheme, which shows up remarkably well in this old black-and-white photograph, albeit in shades of black, white, and gray. The purpose of the contrasting paint scheme was to highlight all of the various architectural details. (MDAH.)

According to the National Register of Historic Places nomination for the Millsaps-Buie House, the date for the major exterior remodeling was 1928. The major change to the Millsaps-Buie House was the replacement of the one-story porch with the giant portico of four Roman Ionic columns. The taste for classical, monumental architecture became extremely popular in Jackson after the completion of the Beaux-Arts–style new capitol building in 1903. This preference began to be seen more and more along North State Street as new houses were built and older ones enlarged and remodeled. With increasing frequency, two-story-high columns of elaborate design (such as the columns added here to the Millsaps-Buie House), along with complete classical entablatures and many other elaborate classically derived architectural details, appeared on North State Street domestic architecture. (MDAH.)

The Marcellus Green House, which stood at 633 North State Street, is shown here after being gutted by fire in April 1966. A date of construction of 1837 was given for the house in an article written in 1936 for the WPA. The original house consisted of six rooms: three per floor, with two in front flanking a central stair hall and a two-story rear ell with one room per floor. The front door surrounds on the facade appear to be in the Greek Revival style popular in the antebellum period. The house underwent major remodeling around the dawn of the 20th century when several rooms were added to the rear, including a new stair hall, and all of the rooms were remodeled. The entrance porch may have been remodeled at this time as well. The windows on the second floor flanking the balcony door are lower than the two in the outer bays, indicating a much larger and different porch arrangement. (St. Andrew's Episcopal School.)

In January 1950, the Marcellus Green House became Green Hall, the new home of St. Andrew's Episcopal School. St. Andrew's School was established in 1947 and opened in the Parish Hall of St. Andrew's Church. The history of the acquisition and remodeling of this stately old home into a school is thoroughly documented in Sherwood Wise's book on the history of the school, *St. Andrew's Episcopal School: A Case for Continuity and Stability in Christian Values*. These photographs, taken in the early 1960s, show the house in use as a school. Still visible, however, are the elegant architectural details added to the house during its *c*. 1900 remodeling. The school continued to use Green Hall and another house next door until the fire in April 1966. The remains of the house were demolished soon thereafter. (Both St. Andrew's Episcopal School.)

According to the National Register of Historic Places nomination for the Garner Wynn Green House, this elegant residence was built in 1910 to the designs of local architect Emmett Hull. This Classical Revival house is one of the finest of its style and period remaining in Jackson. While it is significant for its architecture alone, the history of the family of its builder gives it added significance. Its builder, Garner Wynn Green, was the grandson of one of Jackson's early settlers, Joshua Green, who arrived in the community from Maryland in 1835. Green was a successful businessman, establishing a bank and other business interests. His son, Marcellus Green, lived in the house formerly located at 633 North State Street and was himself a successful businessman and attorney. Garner Wynn Green was also a successful attorney, who was acknowledged as the dean of Mississippi lawyers during his long and exceptional career. This house is located at 647 North State Street. (MDAH.)

Not all of the houses that once stood along North State Street were grand Classical Revival mansions like the Garner Wynn Green residence or impressive Greek Revival structures like the Hilzheim-Ledbetter House. Quite a number of the houses were smaller, simpler cottages. This democratic mix of grand mansions and smaller houses contributed much to the interest of the street. This raised, galleried cottage was located at 702 North State Street, on the northeast corner of its intersection with George Street. The photograph below is of the owner of the house, a Mr. Williams. Apparently someone was fond of gardening, given the large number of plants visible on the porch behind Williams. (Both MDAH.)

Occupied by Greenbrook Flowers since 1963, the Crowder-Capers House, located at 705 North State Street, was the childhood home of Charlotte Capers, third director of the MDAH. Constructed around 1894, this house is one of the few remaining in the Queen Anne style along North State Street. This interpretation of the style, combining classically inspired details with the irregularity of form and shape most commonly associated with the Queen Anne style, such as the steep roof, projecting gable, and round and square corner towers, is often referred to as Queen Anne Free Classic. Later changes made to convert the house to commercial use caused the loss of many of the original features of the house. From about 1850 to 1871, this entire block was the Yerger Estate. (Both MDAH.)

The Beard House, formerly located at 715 North State Street, was a picturesque example of the Classical Revival style. Attributed to Theodore Link, the architect of the 1903 new capitol, this house employed richly detailed Corinthian columns on its ample front porch. Other classically inspired details included Palladian windows in the gables on both the facade and northern elevation, paired consoles that support the cornice returns on the front roof gable, and a bold, denticulated cornice that encircled the house at both the eaves and at second-floor level. Even though the house employed an asymmetrical floor plan typical of the earlier Queen Anne style, this house overall took a much more serious approach to classicism. This elegant house was demolished in the 1980s. The site is now a vacant lot. (Both MDAH.)

Formerly located at 726 North State Street, the Frank Neal House, also known as the Worley House, was a large two-and-one-half-story Classical Revival house. Constructed around 1900, this house was fronted by a two-story gallery that wrapped around a two-story projecting bay on the facade. The columns supporting this gallery appear to have been of a simple Tuscan style linked together by a balustrade of turned spindles. The hipped roof, crowned with decorative iron cresting, was further embellished by several gabled dormers. According to a report written around 1980 by an architectural historian with the MDAH, this house was "the best on its block." Unfortunately, that was not enough to save it. It was demolished on April 15, 1980. (Both MDAH.)

The Merrill-Maley House, located at 735 North State Street, is seen here on March 5, 1940, after a snowstorm. According to the National Register of Historic Places nomination for the house, the land was acquired in 1907 by Phillip S. Merrill, the manager of the George B. Merrill and Brothers Lumber Company. Merrill built the house shortly thereafter as his family home. This imposing Classical Revival house is dominated by its grand portico of two-story Corinthian columns arranged in groups of three on each corner. The architectural detailing on this two-story frame house is in the bold classically influenced style common for this style and period. Notable are the large-scale modillion cornice and the bas-relief carved wooden panels filling the space between the first- and second-floor tripartite windows. The elegant house was crowned with an elaborate, green, glazed tile roof. (MDAH.)

These houses, on the east side of the 800 block of North State Street, date to the early 20th century. The house at left is an American Four Square with Classical Revival detailing. An American Four Square is a house form two stories high, square in shape, and characterized by asymmetrical floor plans reflected in asymmetrical facades. The house below is another simplified version of the Classical Revival style. This two-story gable-front house with a full two-story double-tiered gallery of square tapered columns embodies the basic form of the Classical Revival style with the simplest of materials and ornamentation. (Both MDAH.)

According to *Jackson Landmarks*, the Ligon-Gale House, located at 839 North State Street, was constructed around 1870 by Sarah Moseley Ligon and her husband, John. The residence was sold in 1897 to Anne Sue Gale. It was apparently Gale who remodeled the house, adding its extravagant Classical Revival gallery. This gallery is composed of fluted Corinthian columns sitting atop paneled bases linked by heavy turned balusters. The gallery sits atop a rusticated stone foundation wall that serves as a visual contrast to the elegance of the columns and other details. The gallery roof is visually supported on the facade of the house by Corinthian pilasters. A similar balustrade tops the gallery roof as well as a small, flat-roofed platform atop the low pitched, hipped roof. The center entrance is flanked by Corinthian pilasters. An elaborate dormer with a Palladian window on the front slope of the roof is barely visible behind the roof balustrade. Visible on the right of the photograph is the Virden-Fagan House. (LBHF.)

The Virden-Fagan House, situated at 901 North State Street, was constructed around 1912. The design of this grand Classical Revival house has been attributed to new capitol architect Theodore Link. If Link was indeed the architect for this house, as well as the Beard House at 715 North State Street and the Daniel Wilkinson House at 204 North State Street, then he was among the most talented designers of his day. The Virden-Fagan House, a two-and-one-half-story frame structure, is dominated by a grand colonnade of two-story Corinthian columns topped by a well-proportioned entablature. Atop the colonnade is a balustrade composed of a wooden railing separated by paneled piers. The railing is composed of a crisscross design reminiscent of the Union Jack flag. Visible through the balustrade in the large front gable is an elaborate Palladian window lighting the top story. (MDAH.)

This postcard view of the east side of the 900 block of North State Street shows how the street looked in the early 20th century. The house to the right is the R. L. Saunders House. The house next door, previously located at 918 North State Street, is the S. J. Johnson House. Built around 1890, it was an elegant example of the Queen Anne Free Classic style. (Mrs. Samuel Fletcher King.)

The R. L. Saunders House, formerly located at 906 North State Street, was an elegant *c.* 1896 Colonial Revival house. This house was heavily decorated with classically inspired details, from the Ionic porch columns, to the heavy modillion cornice. The centerpiece of the southern elevation was a large-scale Palladian window lighting the stair landing. There was also a grand porte cochere on the southern elevation. (Mrs. Samuel Fletcher King.)

This photograph shows the Saunders family in front of their home. The architect was William C. Weston, an architect from Chicago who had been involved with the construction of many of the buildings and exhibits at the Columbian Exposition of 1893. The baby is Mrs. Samuel Fletcher King, the donor of the photograph. (Mrs. Samuel Fletcher King.)

According to an article from the *Jackson Daily News* in 1935, Jackson's street railway began in 1871 using mule-drawn cars like the one seen in this photograph, which was taken on North State Street. On August 1, 1899, the mule-drawn cars were replaced with electric streetcars, which were themselves replaced by buses on March 24, 1935. (LBHF.)

Fortification Street, the location of Civil War–era fortifications, is shown in the above *c.* 1930 photograph looking toward its intersection with North State Street. The building visible in the distance is the First Church of Christ, Scientist. Apparently the purpose of this photograph, taken by the City of Jackson, was to show the condition of the streets, gutters, and sidewalks here along Fortification Street. The photograph below, dating from about 10 years later, provides a closer view of the *c.* 1925 eclectic Craftsman/Tudor Revival–style Christian Science church. The church was later converted to commercial purposes and was demolished in the 1990s after being damaged by fire. (Above, LBHF; below, MDAH.)

This building, erected in 1881 as the main building for the Mississippi School for the Blind, was designed by architect Alfred Zucker in an elaborate late-19th-century eclectic style. While both of these photographs may at first appear to be the same, these images show a change made to the building. The photograph above shows the tower after it was shortened from its original height, as seen in the photograph below, by the removal of the columns that originally supported the steeply pitched roof of the tower. The first school for the blind was established in Jackson in 1847 through the efforts of James Champlin, a blind philanthropist from Sharon, Mississippi. During the Civil War, the school moved to Monticello but moved back to Jackson in 1881 to the new campus. (Both MDAH.)

The Mississippi School for the Blind remained on this site for the next 70 years. As the years passed, new buildings were erected to provide for the school's increasing student population. These photographs show the new boys' dormitory under construction in the 1930s. The simple dignified design of this two-story, brick, Georgian Revival–style building, designed in 1934 by the Jackson architectural firm of Hull and Drummond, provided quite a contrast with the elaborate late-19th-century exuberance of Zucker's main building, seen in the photograph above to the right. (Both MDAH.)

Noah Webster Overstreet, one of Mississippi's most prolific 20th-century architects, designed this auditorium around 1916 for the school for the blind. The overhanging eaves, paired brackets, and low pitched, hipped, tile roof all contribute to its Prairie-style design. Surviving the demolition of the rest of the campus when the school moved in the 1950s, the auditorium was demolished by the Mississippi Baptist Medical Center in May 1984. (MDAH.)

This photograph shows the State Charity Hospital shortly after it was completed in 1912. The hospital, formerly located at 1219 North State Street, stood where the current Baptist Hospital stands. The charity hospital was demolished in the early 1950s after the University Medical Center opened and took over the role filled for many years by this institution. (LBHF.)

Beth Israel Cemetery occupies the west side of the 1300 block of North State Street. According to *Jackson Landmarks*, this cemetery was deeded to the Hebrew congregation of Jackson in 1860. This early date makes Beth Israel Cemetery, although outside the city limits at the time it was begun, one of the earliest cemeteries in Jackson. Greenwood Cemetery was the first burial ground in Jackson and dates to the 1820s. It too was outside the city limits at the time it began. The Congregation Beth Israel was officially organized in 1861. The Congregation's current synagogue on Old Canton Road is at least its third. Previous locations were on Woodrow Wilson Avenue west of North State Street from 1941 to 1967 and prior to that at the southeast corner of South and South State Streets from 1875 to 1940. (Both MDAH.)

Power School, formerly located at the southeast corner of North State and Pinehurst Streets, was constructed in 1916. The brick with stone trim, two-story-over-basement, Prairie-style school sat back from North State Street on a slight rise, adding prominence to its impressive design. The photograph above shows the building from North State Street. The lower photograph, taken on November 10, 1938, shows the northern elevation of the school and gives a better idea of the size of the structure. According to the *Survey of the Schools of Hinds County, Mississippi*, published in 1917, the Power School was the "latest addition to Jackson's school system . . . and represents an expenditure of $30,000." The school was named for Col. John L. Power, a former secretary of state. (Above, MDAH; below, LBHF.)

The Queen Anne–style house seen in this photograph was constructed as the home of the William Hamilton Watkins family around 1900. This house was originally located at 1423 North State Street. It was moved to this location at 620 Webster Street when, according to the inscription on the back of the photograph, the "big house was built." The "big house" was the Classical Revival house constructed by W. H. and Margaret Watkins in 1908–1909. While moving houses to save them from demolition for historic preservation purposes is a fairly common practice today, they were often moved in the past simply because it made economic sense given the expense and care that went into their construction. Moving a house that was at most 10 years old just around the corner made sense. Unfortunately, this move did not preserve the house forever. The Queen Anne structure was gone by 1962. At least two other houses on North State Street were moved to save them from demolition and then given a new use. (MDAH.)

This photograph, made around 1935, shows the Classical Revival–style W. H. Watkins House that was built in 1908–1909 at 1423 North State Street on the location of the house shown on page 65. The removal of what was essentially a brand-new house shows how quickly fashions change. The Queen Anne house that was moved around the corner to the southwest, while certainly elegant, well designed, and substantial, was apparently just too old fashioned for the Watkinses by 1908. Rather than remodel their existing house, as the Millsaps did at 628 North State Street, they replaced it. Certainly, this Classical Revival house was one of the most substantial and elegant of the classically inspired houses built along North State Street. Its hilltop location gave increased prominence to the architecturally impressive structure. (MDAH.)

The dual projecting porticos at the north and south ends of the Roman Ionic colonnade of the W. H. Watkins House were unique on North State Street. The porticos not only had pediments on the facade, but also on the north and south elevations, which, along with the engaged columns supporting the roof of the colonnade at the front wall of the house, gave increased prominence to these secondary elevations. Centered on the facade between the two projecting porticos was the elegant main entrance. This entrance was crowned by a gracefully arched fanlight, all enclosed within an impressive surround. The tripartite windows on both floors were centered behind the porticos. The photograph at right shows an elegantly attired Mrs. Watkins in her new home. The house burned around 1984. (Both MDAH.)

The McIntyre House, located at 1438 North State Street, was constructed around 1925 in an eclectic style popular in the 1920s and 1930s. The round arched windows, low pitched, hipped roof covered with clay tiles, asymmetrically placed chimneys, and masonry exterior all contributed to the picturesque Mediterranean style that was so popular at the time. (MDAH.)

Constructed around 1922, the Adams-Connor House at 1535 North State Street is one of the most unique houses on the street. The horizontal emphasis, a hallmark of the Prairie style, is evident in the heavy cornice that wraps around the main body of the house and the projecting wings. The long, narrow windows with decorative upper muntins are another hallmark of this style. (MDAH.)

The Barksdale House, located at 1440 North State Street, was constructed around 1910. This Classical Revival house is dominated by its colonade of Roman Ionic columns. The asymmetrical first floor of the facade contrasts with the symmetry of the columns as well as the symmetry of the second floor and the centered, cantilevered balcony. (MDAH.)

Located at 1505 North State Street, the Flowers-McLaurin House, constructed around 1905, has one of the most architecturally sophisticated Craftsman-style facades in Jackson. The broad eaves with paired brackets, patterned window sash, and large battered piers that support the entrance porch and side porches are all hallmarks of this style. (MDAH.)

The Mims House, constructed around 1905 and located at 1530 North State Street, is seen here in a photograph taken not long after its completion. The house is designed in the Classical Revival style. The house's most distinctive feature is its front colonnade composed of two-story-tall Corinthian columns topped by an imposing Corinthian entablature. Crowning the colonnade is a balustrade composed of turned balusters linking paneled piers placed directly above the columns. Lighting the top floor is a large dormer with a Palladian window. While the treatment of the columns, separated into pairs at each end of the colonnade with a much wider opening between, is not classically correct in the strictest of terms, it does employee the symmetry so important in classical architecture. The railing of the balcony over the entrance is supported on paired consoles. The symmetry of the balcony, located above the off-center main entrance, mirrors the symmetry of the facade. (Mrs. Robert B. Mims.)

Located at 1515 North State Street, the Lampton-Wallace House, now known as the McRae House, was constructed around 1913. This redbrick two-story house is designed in the Georgian Revival style. The monumental Classical Revival style that had dominated high-style architecture for the first decade of the 20th century was not an attempt to re-create any specific architecture of the past but rather revive it in a new age. The Lampton-Wallace House represents a change in American architecture as architects began to look for inspiration in America's historic buildings. This house is an early-20th-century interpretation of the large brick mansions built during the 18th century in Virginia and Maryland. According to *Jackson Landmarks*, the first occupant of this house was Thad Lampton, who served as state treasurer. The Junior Auxiliary of Jackson, now the Junior League, was organized in this house in 1927. (MDAH.)

The Lawrence-Farrington-Young House, located at 1543 North State Street, was constructed in 1927 to the designs of architect Claude H. Lindsley. This house, like the Lampton-Wallace-McRae House, was designed and built in the Georgian Revival style. The centrally located entrance, surmounted by an elliptical fanlight and flanked by sidelights, is sheltered by a portico supported by Tuscan columns clustered at the corners. The portico roof is crowned by a balustrade. The facade is framed by corner quoins, and the eaves are decorated with a modillion cornice. Centered on the front slope of the low pitched, hipped roof is a single dormer with a Palladian window. The lot where this house sits is right next door to the Millsaps College campus. Originally on the site was a smaller house, built around 1905, that was once occupied by the president of Millsaps. (MDAH.)

According to *Jackson, A Special Kind of Place*, Founder's Hall (seen here in an early photograph) was constructed around 1885 for Jackson College. Jackson College began in 1877 in Natchez as the Natchez Seminary and moved to Jackson in 1883. Millsaps College, organized on January 10, 1890, and named in honor of Maj. R. W. Millsaps after he made a generous donation toward the establishment of the college, held its first session on September 29, 1892, on a site immediately adjacent to the campus of Jackson College. After 10 years of existing side by side, Jackson College sold its land to Millsaps College. Jackson College then moved to its new campus west of downtown on Lynch Street. Jackson College is today Jackson State University. Founder's Hall was used by Millsaps College for many years. This three-story brick building thus had the distinction of serving two of Jackson's institutions of higher learning. (MDAH.)

Taken in 1929, this photograph shows the new fire station located on North State Street. The fire station was built sometime after 1925 and before 1929. The tall vertical structure seen to the left was the standpipe or water tower. The city acquired this property, at the time described as the southeast corner of the intersection of North State Street and Woodrow Wilson Avenue, in 1928 and developed a small park. Standpipe Park functioned primarily as a landscaped garden and passive recreation area. The area around the new fire station has the raw look of a new development. Note the small saplings in front of the fire station. Barely visible in the right edge of the photograph is the northern wall of a small commercial building, constructed about the same time as the fire station and no doubt serving as a neighborhood grocery or the like given the considerable distance from downtown. Riverside Drive was not yet constructed. (LBHF.)

This photograph was taken on April 15, 1939, at least 10 years after the photograph on the opposite page. The small sapling in the first photograph has grown quite a bit. The fire station was designed in a simplified Mission Revival style, one of many revival styles popular in the 1920s and 1930s, with its stucco surface, arched openings, and tile roof designed to recall the Spanish missions of the Colonial Southwest. Of course, the dominant element in the photograph is the fire engine and the members of this station, which by this time was identified as the No. 5 Fire Station. The firemen are, from left to right, G. H. Taylor, E. P. Smith, F. H. Sproles, F. D. Robinson, A. B. Boyles, and J. L. Griffin. This building was replaced with a new fire station in 1957. There is also a new water tower on the site of the old standpipe. (LBHF.)

This elegant Classical Revival mansion, constructed or heavily remodeled around 1910, is not located on a large private estate but was the residence for the superintendent of the State Insane Asylum and was located on the asylum property. The original photograph identifies the house as "Dr. Mitchell's House." A Dr. Mitchell was superintendent at least as early as 1927. In a promotional publication released in 1927 called *The Book of Jackson*, Dr. C. D. Mitchell was praised for his guidance and was called a "progressive superintendent." Apparently his leadership was valued because he shows up in the 1930 and 1937 city directories as superintendent of the hospital. Unfortunately, however, the antebellum facility located on North State Street was demolished upon the completion of the new hospital, which was erected in Rankin County. (MDAH.)

Three

THE MODERN ERA

Jackson continued to grow during the 1920s. By 1930, Jackson finally surpassed Meridian to become Mississippi's largest community. To meet the needs for housing during the Great Depression and the years of World War II, some of the grand old homes along North State Street were converted to boardinghouses. The first apartment buildings began to appear in the 1920s and 1930s cheek-by-jowl with the grand old mansions.

After World War II, Jackson, a 19th-century town, became a 20th-century city. During the 1950s, North State Street changed from a predominantly residential street of fine houses occupied by the first families of the community to a street of much less exclusionary uses. The decay and neglect of two decades of depression and war gave way to promises of a gleaming future. Changes in taste and zoning, and an increase in traffic on North State Street, which by now was an increasingly busy U.S. Highway 51, all combined to contribute to the loss or severe alteration of many of these stately mansions. One by one, they fell victim to progress.

Although not as universally loved as the grand old houses, some of the new buildings erected along North State Street during this period are among the best of their time and place, and were designed by prominent architects, some of whom gained worldwide fame for their work. For example, Bailey Junior High School attracted international attention in the late 1930s for being the world's first school constructed of steel-reinforced concrete. The building's architects, N. W. Overstreet and Hays Town, enjoyed the fame generated from this building for years to come.

The photograph above was taken in February 1950 from the middle of the intersection of Capitol and President Streets looking toward the Old Capitol. The Old Capitol stands as it had for more than 100 years looking down the street that shared its name. The Old Capitol had been converted into a state office building in 1917 and still served this purpose at the time of this photograph. The photograph below, taken from the balcony of the Old Capitol, looks back down Capitol Street about a decade later. Spengler's Corner, at the time of this photograph the home of Hemphill Drugs, still retains the basic exterior form it had attained approximately 100 years before. This photograph dates to after 1956, the date of construction of the First National Bank, now Trustmark, visible near the center of the photograph. (Both LBHF.)

From 1959 to 1961, after 42 years as offices for various state agencies, the Old Capitol building was restored and converted into the state history museum. The major interior spaces, such as the House and Senate Chambers, were restored as nearly as possible to the way they appeared in the 19th century when the building served as the state capitol. The offices were not restored but instead were renovated to serve as exhibit space for the state history museum. The exterior of the building had been covered with stucco since its completion in 1840. However, during the 1959–1961 restoration, there was a deeply held, although factually incorrect, belief by some involved in the restoration that the building had not been covered with stucco at first or that perhaps William Nichols's original plans did not include such a treatment. (MDAH.)

With the changes made to the portico's entrance in the 1871 renovations, from flat openings to arches, and with its stucco removed in 1959–1961, the Old Capitol resembled Nichols's earlier design for the state capitol in Tuscaloosa, Alabama. Thus Nichols's Greek Revival capitol, designed and constructed in the late 1830s, had by the early 1960s been made to look like a late-1820s Federal-style building. (LBHF.)

This aerial view of downtown Jackson was taken sometime after the restoration of the Old Capitol. The commercialism of downtown can be seen moving up North State Street. The Standard Oil Company building at the corner of Amite and North State Streets was constructed in 1925. Next up the street is the c. 1950 YWCA, and next to that was the 1946 Sears, Roebuck, and Company department store. (LBHF.)

State Street has long been a part of the main parade route through downtown Jackson. These photographs, taken December 9, 1948, show that year's Christmas parade as it winds past the 100 block of North State Street. The Tucker Printing Company buildings, seen near the middle of the photograph above, still retain their early-20th-century Colonial Revival storefronts, soon to disappear in a remodeling to bring them "up to date." Visible in the distance is the steeple of the 1890s First Presbyterian Church, which would also soon disappear. The windows of the second floor of Spengler's Corner are clearly visible on the left below. (Both LBHF.)

This photograph shows Spengler's Corner after a "restoration" attempt made in the late 1970s. At first glance, it is almost impossible to realize that this is the same building as shown in the two 1948 photographs on page 81. Unfortunately, this structure, the oldest extant commercial building in downtown Jackson and dating to the 1840s and 1850s, was subjected to an insensitive and inappropriate remodeling in the 1970s. All of the historic photographs of this building show the windows on the upper floor to have been composed of sash with fewer glass panes than those shown here. The original windows were also composed of double-hung sash, not the triple-hung seen in this photograph. Also, the storefront treatment shown here is not appropriate for the building. The main entrance is especially inappropriate for a commercial building, being much more domestic in scale and design. Unfortunately, this poor building has been subjected to even more inappropriate alterations since this photograph was made. (MDAH.)

This photograph, taken around 1950, looks north up State Street from its intersection with Capitol Street. Visible on the northwest corner of the intersection is Spengler's Corner. This photograph clearly shows the chamfered corner entrance and the large plate-glass display windows most likely added to the building in the 1930s. (LBHF.)

This photograph shows the intersection of North State and Amite Streets looking east toward the fairgrounds. This photograph, taken by the city on August 28, 1947, apparently to document road work, provides an unexpected glimpse into the city's past. Visible in this photograph are the Standard Oil Company building on the left, built in 1927, and the War Memorial Building on the right, completed in 1940. (LBHF.)

In 1934, according to *Mississippi's Old Capitol: Biography of a Building*, the legislature designated the northern end of the Old Capitol Green as a "perpetual memorial to the veterans of World War I." The southern end of the Old Capitol Green had been known since 1891, when the Confederate Memorial was dedicated, as Confederate Park. This, combined with the Spanish War monument erected in front of the Old Capitol in the 1920s, essentially made the entire Old Capitol Green a memorial park. In 1938, the legislature appropriated $150,000 to build a "War Memorial Building" on the northern end of the green. The building was to serve a double purpose: a memorial to Mississippi's veterans and offices for veterans' organizations. In addition, the northern wing of the building was occupied by the Department of Archives and History. Ironically, its completion in 1940 meant that veterans of World War II were not memorialized in this building. Elevator doors dedicated to World War II battles were installed after the war's end. (MDAH.)

The War Memorial Building was designed by Jackson architect E. L. Malvaney in an elegant version of the art deco style often used for government buildings in the 1930s. This style combined the flat two-dimensional abstraction of forms common to the art deco style with the formality and symmetry of classical architecture. This rendering clearly shows the memorial character of the building. All of the decoration had a purpose—to honor Mississippi's veterans. This also shows a proposed reflecting pool that was to be erected in front of the building. Most likely because of funding constraints and materials and labor shortages caused by World War II, the area remained an open grass lawn. The lower drawing shows a preliminary version of the design, not nearly as successful as the executed design. (Both MDAH.)

The Standard Oil Company building, completed by 1927 on the northeast corner of North State and Amite Streets, stands on the site formerly occupied by the Wilkinson House and in the mid-19th century the Bowman House hotel. This view of the Standard Oil Company building shows the North State Street elevation in use, as it had been since its was constructed, as a gas station. The station shown in this c. 1965 photograph had been changed from its original appearance probably about 1960. The Italian Renaissance Revival style of the main building offers an interesting contrast with the mid-20th-century modern station below. This station was one of three service stations located at the intersection of North State and Amite Streets. (LBHF.)

The Standard Oil Company building, designed in the Italian Renaissance Revival style, was completed in 1927. The Italian Renaissance Revival style, one of many eclectic revival styles popular in the 1920s and 1930s, invoked images of Italian palazzos of Renaissance Italy and employed stucco wall surfaces, low pitched tile roofs with wide overhanging eaves, and decorative classically inspired details in stone or terra-cotta. After Standard Oil vacated the building, a new addition accommodating additional offices was constructed on the site of the former service station. This addition is visible in the photograph below. While it does have stucco walls and a tile roof, the addition does not live up to the elegance of the original building. (Above, LBHF; below, MDAH.)

This photograph, made in the 1930s, shows the Wilkinson House, formerly on the northeast corner of Amite and North State Streets, after it was moved to the state fairgrounds to become the women's building. It must have been an elegant place for the ladies visiting the fair, offering the amenity of telephone service, identified by the small Bell Telephone sign hanging on the bay window near the center of the photograph. Amazingly, the house seems to be no worse for the wear after its move down the hill and across Amite Street from its original location. The house is being painted and some basic repairs made. To emphasize the elegant architectural details of the Renaissance Revival–style house, the details have been accented with a contrasting color. This structure remained one of architect Theodore Link's most impressive essays in domestic architecture. (LBHF.)

Taken in March 1935, this view of the flooded fairgrounds shows the former Wilkinson House. The house's western elevation, which originally faced North State Street, now faced the exuberant art deco entrance gates to the state fairgrounds. What was originally the rear of the house now faced up Jefferson Street. The house was apparently demolished around 1950 after Jefferson Street was extended to the south. (LBHF.)

The former Young Women's Christian Association building, 226 North State Street, was constructed around 1950 in a simplified Georgian Revival style. The brick veneer building is virtually devoid of ornament except for the cast-stone door surround with broken pediment, simple cast-stone window trim, and a simple cast-stone cornice. (LBHF.)

Taken after a snowstorm, this photograph shows some of the details of the *c.* 1893 First Presbyterian Church, which stood at 301 North State Street, on the northwest corner of North State and Yazoo Streets, until it was demolished in about 1951. This elegant Gothic Revival building displayed elegant brick detailing, stone trim, and many impressive stained-glass windows. While the exact date of this photograph is not known, it appears to be from the 1940s. It could even be taken after the snowstorm documented in several other photographs that occurred in March 1940. At any rate, this street scene shows a view along North State Street that was not to survive much longer. The congregation of First Presbyterian Church soon built a new home farther up the street, and this venerable old structure was demolished. The houses to the north of the church would also be demolished before too long. (LBHF.)

Sometime after the First Presbyterian Church moved to a new church after its completion in 1951, the 1893 building was demolished. This demolition is documented in these two photographs. The elegant, substantial church slowly gave way to the never-ending wheels of "progress." The stained-glass windows have been removed, as has most of the roofing, but the noble form and proportions of the structure can still be appreciated. The side porch, visible in the snowstorm photograph on page 90, is shown in the photograph below. (Both MDAH.)

An article in the Jackson *Clarion Ledger* on September 2, 1945, explains that very soon the "Old Robinson Home" located at the corner of North State and Mississippi Streets was to be demolished and replaced by a modern business structure. According to this article, "the property was purchased last year [1944] by the Sears, Roebuck and Co. and the old house must make way for the new buildings." The old Robinson house (see page 15) stood on the site of the parking lot for the new store, shown in this *c.* 1946 photograph. Visible just above the roof of the department store is the top of the house, now the site of the former YWCA, at the southeast corner of North State and Yazoo Streets (see page 38). Representing a new age and the changes soon to come to North State Street, this building was a handsome art moderne commercial building. With its clean surfaces and long horizontal lines, it was the epitome of the modern retail experience. It is now the Eudora Welty Library. (Sears Holdings Historical Archives.)

JACKSON MUNICIPAL LIBRARY   JACKSON, MISSISSIPPI

Jackson's new Municipal Library was erected in 1954 at 301 North State Street, the northwest corner of its intersection with Yazoo Street. This site was the location of the 1846 and 1893 First Presbyterian Churches. N. W. Overstreet, one of Mississippi's most prolific architects, was hired to design the new library. Overstreet was also the architect of Jackson's first library building, formerly located at the northwest corner of Mississippi and Congress Streets. The library is very much as the original design (above) intended, except that the entrance was moved to the southernmost bay and the signage was moved to the wall to the left. The entire front elevation was also shortened by two bays. (Above, Overstreet Architectural Records, Special Collections Department, Mitchell Memorial Library, Mississippi State University; below, MDAH.)

The library was designed in a style that can most accurately be called classical modern. The limestone building has no exterior decoration except for the widow and door bays. These bays are visually brought out from the facade and separated by thin vertical members into a simple abstraction of a classical temple front. When lit from within and viewed at night, as seen in the photograph above, this effect is particularly striking. The interior was designed and finished in a completely modern, elegant, and sophisticated manner. The photograph below shows the first-floor reading room looking toward the circulation desk from the entrance. (Above, LBHF; below, MDAH.)

These photographs of the interior of the Municipal Library, created shortly after the building was completed, were taken by a photographer hired by the city. The photograph above shows the second-floor reading room. The most striking architectural feature of this space is the interior balconies shown along the front window wall to the right. The photograph below is of the children's section of the library, located on the first floor. Just visible through the windows on the right side of the photograph is the facade of the YWCA building. (Both MDAH.)

The Clifton-Burwell House, located at 500 North State Street, was in stark contrast to the new commercial and institutional activity taking place just down the street. One of the oldest residences in town, this house began to decline as the character of North State Street changed around it. The house was severely damaged by fire in 1990. Many citizens thought the fire damage would be used as an excuse to demolish the building and replace it with a parking lot, the same fate that had befallen so many other fine structures. Thankfully, through the efforts of local preservationists, it was restored, and today it is an office building. (Both MDAH.)

Seemingly oblivious to all that has happened around it, the Virden-Patton House, at 512 North State Street, has survived for more than 150 years with very few changes. In fact, this house is one of only two or three houses on North State Street south of Fortification Street still occupied as a residence. The photograph at right shows a detail of the fine Greek Revival entrance to the house. Interestingly, this photograph also shows one of the few changes to the house. The house had been painted or stuccoed at least since the 1930s and probably even longer than that. It has had that covering removed. (Both MDAH.)

Formerly located at the northwest corner of North State and High Streets, the Young Man's Christian Association (YMCA) building was constructed sometime after 1949. According to *Lost Mansions of Mississippi*, that was the year the YMCA purchased the Nugent-Shands House (see page 19). The original house was demolished sometime before 1960. Apparently, this modern building was originally built as a rear wing to the Nugent-Shands House. This structure was a modern institutional building for its day. The contrasting brick work, aluminum-framed hopper windows, and the vertical tower-like element, seen above supporting the signage for the YMCA, are all hallmarks of mid-20th-century modern architecture. The confident modernism of this building is an interesting contrast to the architecture of the old YWCA (see page 89). (Above, LBHF; below, MDAH.)

The former First Christian Church, located at 600 North State Street, on the northeast corner of State and High Streets, was constructed around 1949. This building was the fourth home of the Christian church. Their three previous buildings were all located on the northeast corner of Mississippi and North President Streets. After the new church was completed, the congregation sold the old property to the First Baptist Church. The North State Street building is an ambitious mid-20th-century version of Gothic Revival architecture built of yellow brick with stone trim, employing pointed arch windows and dominated by a four-story tower with a spire. While certainly not an archaeologically correct copy of a medieval cathedral or English parish church, this building was clearly meant to continue those building traditions in the modern world. (MDAH.)

The Garner Wynn Green House was listed on the National Register of Historic Places in November 1985. However, since such a listing does nothing to protect privately owned property from demolition, the owner, the Mississippi Bar Association, announced plans to demolish the historic house and build a new office building on the site. This was particularly ironic considering that members of the Green family had been lawyers in Jackson for more than 100 years and the builder of this house, Garner Wynn Green, was considered one of the greatest attorneys in the state. Fortunately, the house was not demolished. Instead, in February 1987, it was moved across the street and turned to face back toward its original location. It has been restored and is now used for offices. (Both MDAH.)

On March 10, 1999, the Crowder-Capers House, the home of Greenbrook Flowers since 1963, suffered a devastating fire. Fortunately, the fire was extinguished before the house was completely destroyed. The house was repaired and put back into use by the florist shop, but in the reconstruction, many of the original architectural details lost in the fire were not replicated, but were instead greatly simplified. (MDAH.)

This stretch of North State Street, looking north from its intersection with George Street, shows a crosswalk apparently used by students who attended Jefferson Davis Elementary School, which faces North Congress Street, to cross over North State Street safely as they walked to and from school. This photograph was made on January 16, 1939. (LBHF.)

As Jackson grew during the 1920s and 1930s, there was an increasing need for housing new arrivals. Many residents of North State Street converted their homes into boardinghouses or rented rooms as a way to supplement incomes and keep many of the old places standing. In addition, new apartment houses were built along North State Street. These photographs show two apartment houses built in the 1930s. The photograph above, taken in 1939, shows the apartment building erected at 721 North State Street, a tall, thin building whose awkward proportions are accented by the paired fluted Doric columns flanking the entrance. The photograph below shows a smaller building next door at 733 North State Street, probably built at about the same time. Designed in the Georgian Revival style, this building has much better proportions and a more pleasing sense of scale. (Both MDAH.)

These photographs show the Merrill-Maley House as it was altered to meet the changing needs of its owners. According to the National Register of Historic Places nomination for the house, in the late 1930s, the first floor of the house was converted into a woman's clothing store. This change in use led to the later alteration of the facade when the one-story additions flanking the portico were added. During World War II, the house was the location of the Town Club, a social club catering to servicemen. In 1945, the house was converted into seven small apartments. It continued to function as an apartment house for the next 30 years before reverting to a commercial use. (Both MDAH.)

The photograph above was taken in 1951 of the staff and employees of the Mississippi Hospital and Medical Service in front of its headquarters at 741 North State Street. The headquarters was originally the Frederick Sullens Home, built around 1910. Many of the fine old homes were converted into offices as well as apartments. The photograph below shows a small, one-story office building erected at 812 North State Street for the Life of Georgia. Built around 1955, this small-scale office building, while seeming at first out of place, in fact was soon one of many such buildings taking the place of the grand old houses. (Above, Edward L. Blake and the Mississippi Farm Bureau Federation; below, MDAH.)

The Ligon-Gale House, constructed around 1870 and remodeled in about 1900 (see page 55), is seen here after it became the Municipal Art Gallery. According to *Jackson Landmarks*, the last private owner of the house, Thomas Gale, left the property to the Mississippi Children's Home Society in 1924 with the stipulation that if the society did not use the house as he wished, the property would be given to the city. The society declined the gift, and the house became the property of the City of Jackson. It has since been in use as the Municipal Art Gallery. The photograph below, taken in April 1950, shows some of the ladies of Jackson at the art gallery apparently preparing for an exhibit. (Both LBHF.)

The Municipal Art Gallery underwent many changes during the mid-20th century. As seen here, the Corinthian columns and the porch balustrade have all been removed and replaced with cast-iron posts and railings, and the roof balustrade has been taken down. (MDAH.)

This apartment building, located at 827 North State Street, was erected in 1941. This apartment house was an architecturally sophisticated essay in the art moderne style with its simple unadorned facade, strong horizontal lines, and corner windows. N. W. Overstreet is believed to have been the architect. (MDAH.)

The R. L. Saunders House, once one of the grandest of the mansions along North State Street (see page 57), was moved in the 1920s around the corner to face south on Boyd Street. After its relocation, it was converted into apartments. A brick apartment house was then built on the house's original site. Both structures were demolished for commercial development in the 1980s. (MDAH.)

This photograph was taken on November 16, 1956, at the intersection of North State and Fortification Streets and was made by the city to document work on the city streets and sidewalks. The Christian Science Church is on the corner. The Primos Restaurant was one of several run by the Primos family at the time. The multistory brick building is the old Baptist Hospital. (LBHF.)

What eventually became Baptist Hospital was founded by Dr. J. F. Hunter and Dr. H. R. Shands in 1909 as an eight-bed, privately run hospital located in a c. 1870 galleried cottage on this site (see page 23). In 1914, a brick two-story with basement building was erected to replace the cottage. A floor was added to this building in 1922. A large addition, shown on the right in the photograph above, was erected around 1930. Additions were further made to the building in 1945 and 1955, creating the building shown below. The building was abandoned in 1976 when the new hospital, constructed across North State Street on the site of the former State Charity Hospital (see page 62) was completed. (Both MDAH.)

This Medical Office Building was constructed in 1955 on the southwest corner of the intersection of North State and Manship Streets. It was built on the northern end of the old campus of the Mississippi School for the Blind (see page 60) after that institution had abandoned the site for a new campus in north Jackson. The aluminum-framed hopper windows were modern for the time. The grouping of most of the windows into bands of contrasting brick on each floor between two outer bays of windows enlivens the facade. The entrance level of the building is separated from the upper floors by different cladding materials (the bottom level is clad in marble) as well as a projecting overhang. (LBHF.)

Taken in February 1950, this photograph shows a group of students crossing North State Street with Power Elementary School in the background. The fact that so many students were walking stresses that most of Jackson at the time was still a pedestrian-friendly community. (LBHF.)

The W. H. Watkins House, one of the grandest houses built along North State Street, did not survive "progress," in this case represented by the growth of the medical community around the Baptist Hospital. As this photograph shows, the house was offered for lease before it burned around 1985. A medical office building now stands on the site. (MDAH.)

Completed in 1951 at 1390 North State Street, the current home of the First Presbyterian Church is the third structure to house the congregation. The first two structures both occupied the northwest corner of North State and Yazoo Streets (see pages 14 and 37). According to *Jackson Landmarks*, architect Walter H. Thomas of Philadelphia was the designer of the present building. As seen in the design of the former Christian church, churches built in mid-20th-century Jackson were largely built in traditional styles, despite the fact that many other buildings were designed in more modern styles. The First Presbyterian Church, built in the Georgian Revival style in salmon-colored brick with stone trim, is intended to invoke the church architecture of the mid- and late 18th centuries. The whole composition is focused on the over-large tower and multi-staged steeple. (MDAH.)

The Green Court Apartments, formerly located at 1400 North State Street, were constructed around 1930. The apartments look almost like storybook cottages after they were covered with a blanket of snow in March 1940. This apartment complex was one of several built on North State Street beginning in the 1920s. The Green Court Apartments were designed in the English Tudor Revival style, one of the many popular revival styles of the 1920s and 1930s. The faux half timbering in the clipped gables, grouped windows, and variegated brickwork are all hallmarks of the Tudor Revival style. The complex was demolished in 1988 for a parking lot. (Both MDAH.)

According to *Jackson Landmarks*, the Swearingen-Smith House was built around 1904 and had a front gallery that was later removed. In 1956, it was deeded to the Jackson Wesley Foundation to serve as a Methodist Student Center. In 1976, it became a private residence again. (MDAH.)

According to an article in the *Clarion Ledger* on March 11, 1984, the Morgan Apartments, built in 1951 at 1510 North State Street, were the "talk of the town." This elegant four-story with penthouse art moderne building was said to be the first in town with a central heat and air-conditioning system. It is now an office building. (MDAH.)

Founder's Hall (pictured above) was one of the oldest buildings on the Millsaps College campus when it was demolished in 1973. The building was constructed by Jackson College around 1885 and was sold to Millsaps College in about 1900. This view shows the building shortly before it was demolished. In the early 20th century, Millsaps's main buildings faced West Street. In 1939, Whitworth Hall (pictured below) was built as a women's dormitory and faced North State Street. As West Street declined in the 1970s and 1980s, Millsaps College developed a more impressive entrance to its campus from North State Street. In the 1980s, Whitworth Hall was converted from a dormitory to an administrative building. (Both MDAH.)

This 1938 aerial photograph shows the recently completed Bailey Junior High School. This school was constructed at the northeast corner of North State Street and Riverside Drive. The school was designed by N. W. Overstreet and his partner at the time, Hays Town. Overstreet was one of Mississippi's most respected and accomplished architects in the state at the time he and Town joined forces in the mid-1920s. This building catapulted the firm into national and international prominence thanks in large part to the reinforced-concrete construction of the building. Completed in July 1937 after a year and a half of careful planning and construction, the school cost $350,000. The building is dominated by a tower marking its main entrance. The projecting wing on the south is the auditorium. Contrary to a popular myth, this building was not constructed as a jail. (LBHF.)

In an article written in 1937 for the professional journal *Architectural Concrete*, Hays Town goes into great detail explaining that the decision to use concrete was primarily out of concern for building stability, given the volatility of the yazoo clay so dominant in Jackson. This building was believed to be able to withstand the constant moving of this soil, which has been described as a slow-moving earthquake. (LBHF.)

The other reason given for the use of concrete was for its design potential. Town admitted that the tendency in architecture at the time was toward "a more functional, possibly more severe design" but that such designs were not fully appreciated as was a design of a more conservative, monumental character, which he called "conservative-modern." The tigers flanking this entrance are the school's mascot. This photograph also shows the articulation of the rubbed concreted facade. The half-round cantilevered awning with its incised decoration is also made of concrete. (MDAH.)

This bas-relief panel, next to the steps to the main entrance, depicts the signing of the Treaty of Doak's Stand, the 1820 treaty between the U.S. government and the Choctaw Nation that ceded to the U.S. government more than 5 million acres, including the land on which Jackson was founded. In contrast to the bold, monumental exterior, the interior is a sleek, even elegant, exercise in the art moderne style, shown in the photograph below of the main stair lobby. (Both MDAH.)

Located at 2407 North State Street, on the northwest corner of its intersection with Woodrow Wilson Avenue, the Mississippi Federation of Women's Clubs headquarters was constructed from 1935 to 1937. According to its National Register of Historic Places nomination, this building was erected on land leased from the State of Mississippi and built with assistance from the Works Progress Administration. This Georgian Revival–style building was designed by Jackson architects Robert W. Naef and Associates. The Mississippi Federation of Women's Clubs was organized in Kosciusko in 1898 at a meeting of representatives from women's clubs from Vicksburg, Natchez, Jackson, Okolona, and Meridian. This organization made many contributions to Mississippi in the fields of civic, cultural, educational, and philanthropic activities, and was largely responsible for the formation of the Mississippi Forestry Commission and the State Library Commission. (MDAH.)

This photograph, made by the City of Jackson to document road repairs and construction, was taken in April 1951 at the intersection of North State Street and Woodrow Wilson Avenue looking north. The widening of North State Street was an important part of the development of north Jackson. The property on both sides in the photograph was state property originally belonging to the State Insane Asylum. This property was acquired by the state in the late 1840s for the location of the soon to be constructed hospital for the housing and treatment of the insane. The hospital moved to its new location in Rankin County in 1935. The buildings of the old hospital were abandoned and demolished over the years following the move. This area would soon be the site of the new University of Mississippi Medical Center and many other buildings associated with health care. (LBHF.)

Taken by the City of Jackson in July 1930 to document the condition of the streets and sidewalks in the area, this photograph shows the view south down North State Street from the area of town known as Fondren. Fondren, originally known as Asylum Heights, was once a separate community named after early businessman and resident David Futon Fondren, who, according to *Jackson Landmarks*, opened a grocery store in the area in 1893. In the center of the photograph is visible the dome of the main building of the State Insane Asylum, completed around 1855 (see page 24). (LBHF.)

This *c.* 1950 photograph, taken where Old Canton Road branches off to the east from North State Street, shows one of the last remaining structures from the State Insane Asylum. At the time this photograph was made, the building shown here was in use as state offices. (LBHF.)

By the early 1950s, the last of the old buildings of the insane asylum were all removed, and the land was cleared in preparation for the construction of the new University of Mississippi Medical Center. The cornerstone of the original building was salvaged and taken to the new state hospital at Whitfield, where this photograph was taken. (MDAH.)

Gov. Hugh White, looking grave on this momentous occasion, stands behind the podium ready to speak to the crowd assembled to participate in the ceremonial ground-breaking for the new University of Mississippi Medical Center. Adorning the podium is a handsome rendering of the modern design for the new medical center that would soon rise on the site of the old State Insane Asylum. (Clayton Rand Papers, Special Collections Department, Mitchell Memorial Library, Mississippi State University.)

Shown from left to right are unidentified, Mrs. Hugh (Judith) White, Gov. Hugh White, and Paul B. Johnson Jr. They are shown ceremonially breaking ground for the University Medical Center in 1953. Governor White was at this time serving in his second term as governor. He was elected to his first term in 1935 when he introduced a plan to balance agriculture with industry. (Clayton Rand Papers, Special Collections Department, Mitchell Memorial Library, Mississippi State University.)

The effort to start a medical school in Mississippi began with the establishment of a two-year medical school at the University of Mississippi in Oxford in 1903. In 1908, a school of pharmacy was established in Oxford. An effort was made simultaneously to make it a four-year school. Vicksburg offered its charity hospital as the site for the second half of the proposed four-year school in 1909. Due to lack of funds and equipment, the experiment lasted only one year. Finally, in 1950, the state legislature authorized the establishment of a four-year medical school and teaching hospital in Jackson as a part of the University of Mississippi. The medical center opened on October 24, 1955. The cost was $8.5 million. This aerial photograph was made shortly thereafter. (LBHF.)

This aerial view shows the original hospital with an early wing added at the northeast corner of the building by 1962. The University of Mississippi Medical Center was the site of many firsts in medical history. For example, as listed in *A History of Mississippi, Volume II* (edited by Richard Aubrey McLemore), the University Medical center saw, "The first use of medical anesthesia in 1961; the first human kidney transplant in 1962; the world's first human lung transplant in June 1963; the first adrenal glands transplanted in human beings, also in 1963; the first heart transplant in January, 1964, when a primate heart beat for ninety minutes in the body of a male patient." It may have taken a while to get started, but the University of Mississippi Medical Center has more than lived up to its promise. (LBHF.)

Taken on October 20, 1949, by the City of Jackson to document the condition of streets within the city, this photograph shows Old Canton Road on the right leading off toward some of the most fashionable neighborhoods in Jackson. To the left is North State Street. North State Street, the route of U.S. Highway 51, was the major north-to-south traffic artery through Mississippi at the time. Motorists traveling from Jackson to Memphis or from Jackson to New Orleans would have passed by this intersection. Interstate 55 would parallel this highway to the east just a few years later and would take much of this traffic with it. Fondren, the area of Jackson surrounding this intersection, was on its way to becoming a thriving suburban area of Jackson. In fact, Fondren was the site of the first suburban shopping center constructed in Mississippi. A new age had begun. (LBHF.)

BIBLIOGRAPHY

Brinson, Carroll. *Jackson: A Special Kind of Place*. Jackson, MS: Hederman Brothers, 1977.

From Frontier Capitol to Modern City: A History of Jackson, Mississippi's Built Environment, 1865–1950. Gainesville, GA: Jaeger Company for the City of Jackson, Mississippi, 2000.

Kimbrough, Julie L. *Jackson*. Charleston, SC: Arcadia Publishing, 1998.

McCain, William D. *The Story of Jackson: A History of the Capital of Mississippi 1821–1951*. Jackson, MS: J. F. Hyer Publishing Company, 1953.

McLemore, Richard Aubrey, ed. *A History of Mississippi: Volume I and II*. Hattiesburg, MS: University and College Press of Mississippi, 1973.

Miller, Mary Carol. *Lost Landmarks of Mississippi*. Jackson, MS: University Press of Mississippi, 2002.

———. *Lost Mansions of Mississippi*. Jackson, MS: University Press of Mississippi, 1996.

Skates, John Ray. *Mississippi's Old Capitol: Biography of a Building*. Jackson, MS: MDAH, 1990.

Phillips, Steven J. *Old House Dictionary: An Illustrated Guide to American Domestic Architecture 1600 to 1940*. Lakewood, CO: American Source Books, 1989.

Saylor, Henry H. *Dictionary of Architecture*. New York: John Wiley and Sons, Inc., 1952.

The Junior League of Jackson, Mississippi. *Jackson Landmarks*. Jackson, MS: Calvin Hales Advertising, 1982.

ACROSS AMERICA, PEOPLE ARE DISCOVERING
SOMETHING WONDERFUL. THEIR HERITAGE.

Arcadia Publishing is the leading local history publisher in the United States.
With more than 5,000 titles in print and hundreds of new titles released every
year, Arcadia has extensive specialized experience chronicling the history of
communities and celebrating America's hidden stories, bringing to life the people,
places, and events from the past. To discover the history of other communities
across the nation, please visit:

www.arcadiapublishing.com

Customized search tools allow you to find regional history books about the town
where you grew up, the cities where your friends and family live, the town where
your parents met, or even that retirement spot you've been dreaming about.